First
Facts®

Staying Safe

Staying Safe around Fire

by Lucia Raatma

CAPSTONE PRESS
a capstone imprint

First Facts is published by Capstone Press,
151 Good Counsel Drive, P.O. Box 669, Mankato, Minnesota 56002.
www.capstonepub.com

 Books published by Capstone Press are manufactured with paper
containing at least 10 percent post-consumer waste.

Library of Congress Cataloging-in-Publication Data
Raatma, Lucia.
  Staying safe around fire / by Lucia Raatma.
    p. cm. — (First facts. Staying safe)
  Includes bibliographical references and index.
  Summary: "Discusses rules for fire prevention and safety at home and outdoors"—Provided by
publisher.
  ISBN 978-1-4296-6820-0 (library binding)
  ISBN 978-1-4296-7193-4 (paperback)
  1. Fire prevention—Juvenile literature. 2. Accidents—Prevention—Juvenile literature.
I. Title.
  TH9148.R3322 2012
  628.9'22—dc22   2011003313

Editorial Credits

Rebecca Glaser and Christine Peterson, editors; Ted Williams, designer;
    Svetlana Zhurkin, media researcher; Laura Manthe, production specialist

Photo Credits

Capstone Studio/Karon Dubke, cover, 1, 6–7, 10, 11, 14, 15 (all), 17, 18, 20; Corbis/Rick Gomez,
12–13; iStockphoto/Inga Nielsen, 16; Sean Locke, 8; Shutterstock/Brian McDonald, 5

Essential content terms are **bold** and are defined at the bottom of the spread where they first appear.

Printed in the United States of America in North Mankato, Minnesota.
032011   006110CGF11

Table of Contents

All Kinds of Fires

People use fire in many ways. Campfires keep you warm. Fire from a grill cooks hamburgers. A small candle flame makes your house smell good.

But fires can be dangerous if they are not **controlled**. Uncontrolled fires can damage buildings and harm people. But you can stay safe around fire if you follow the rules.

control—to keep within safe limits

Preventing Fires

Most fires can be prevented. Keep **flammable** objects away from stoves, space heaters, fireplaces, and other heat sources.

flammable—able to burn

Flammable objects, such as paper and clothing, catch fire quickly. Check for flammable objects in your home. Move these items away from heat sources.

Matches and Lighters

Adults use matches and lighters to start fires in fireplaces, grills, and other safe places. But you should never use matches or lighters. You could start a fire by accident. If you find matches or lighters, give them to an adult right away.

Fire Safety in the Kitchen

Have an adult help you in the kitchen. Never put flammable objects on burners or in the oven.

Cooking can cause fires. Turn pot handles toward the center of the stove so they don't get bumped. Ask an adult to keep a **fire extinguisher** in your kitchen.

fire extinguisher—a holder with water or safe chemicals inside it that is used to put out small fires

Outdoor Fires

Outdoor campfires and grills are fun to be around. But don't get too close. You could get burned. Have an adult start campfires and grills. Keep away from outdoor fires, and ask an adult to do the cooking.

Never throw objects into a fire or add **lighter fluid**. The fire could grow and spread quickly.

lighter fluid—a flammable liquid used to light controlled fires

Stop, Drop, and Roll

If you come into contact with fire, remember to stop, drop, and roll. If you or your clothing catch on fire, don't run. Stop what you are doing. Drop to the ground. Roll on the ground until the fire is out. Then find an adult to help you.

15

Smoke Alarms

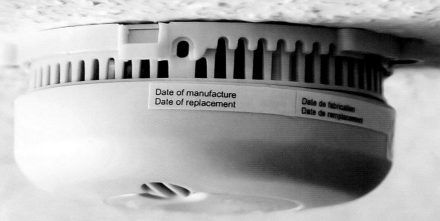

Date of manufacture
Date of replacement

Date de fabrication
Date de remplacement

Smoke alarms help keep you safe if a fire breaks out. These alarms make loud sounds when they sense smoke. The alarm warns you to get out fast.

Ask an adult to put a smoke alarm on each level of your home. Adults should test each smoke alarm once a month. Remind your family to replace smoke alarm batteries twice a year.

Escape Routes

To stay safe during a fire, plan an **escape route** from your house. Find two exits in each room such as doors and windows. Choose a safe family meeting place outside your home. Practice your escape plan several times each year.

escape route—a way to leave a building in an emergency

Safe Escape

If a fire happens, stay calm. Cover your mouth with a shirt or cloth. Crawl toward an exit. Feel a door before opening. If it's hot, there may be fire on the other side. Once you are safe outside, do not go back inside your house. Call 9-1-1 for help.

Hands On:
Plan an Escape Route

An escape route will help your family get out safely in a fire. Meet with your family members to plan and practice an escape route.

What You Need

paper   red marker
black marker   members of your family

What You Do

1. On the paper, use the black marker to draw a map of your home.
2. Circle windows and doors on the map with the red marker. These are exits. Find two exits for every room.
3. With a marker, draw the best way to get out of each room. Everyone should learn two ways out of each room.
4. Choose a place where your family will meet outside. Mark your meeting place on the map.
5. Hold fire drills using different escape routes.

Glossary

control (kuhn-TROHL)—to keep within safe limits

escape route (es-KAYP ROOT)—a way to leave a building in an emergency

fire extinguisher (FYR ik-STING-gwi-shuhr)—a holder with water or safe chemicals inside it that is used to put out small fires

flammable (FLA-muh-buhl)—able to burn

lighter fluid (LY-tur FLOO-id)—a flammable liquid used to light controlled fires; only adults should use lighter fluid

Read More

Barraclough, Sue. *Fire Safety*. Stay Safe. Chicago: Heinemann Library, 2008.

Johnson, Jinny. *Being Safe*. Now We Know about. New York: Crabtree Pub. Co., 2010.

Rau, Dana Meachen. *Fire Safety*. Bookworms: Safe Kids. New York: Marshall Cavendish Benchmark, 2009.

Internet Sites

FactHound offers a safe, fun way to find Internet sites related to this book. All of the sites on FactHound have been researched by our staff.

Here's all you do:

Visit *www.facthound.com*

Type in this code: 9781429668200

Super-cool stuff!

Check out projects, games and lots more at
www.capstonekids.com

Index

My
First
Book of
Nature

Birds

Victoria Munson

WINDMILL
BOOKS

Published in 2019 by Windmill Books,
an Imprint of Rosen Publishing
29 East 21st Street, New York, NY 10010

Editor: Victoria Brooker
Book Design: Elaine Wilkinson

Photo Credits:
All graphics Shutterstock.com, and cover: main
Mark Medcalf tr Menno Schaefer; tl Alexander
Erdbeer; bl Jozef Sowa; br Cric Isselee; 1, 6
Edwin/Butter/; 4 Dominique de La Croix; 5t
ChameleonsEye; 5b dmodlin01; 6b Howard
Marsh; 7t Bruce MacQueen; 7b RT Images; 8l
Marc Goldman; 8r John Navajo; 9t Bildagentur
Zoonar GmbH; 9b Visayas; 10l Zakharov
Aleksey; 10r FotoRequest; 11 Rudmer Zwerver;
12 Belen Bilgic Schneider; 13t Arvind Balaraman;
13b Juan Roballo; 14t MAC1; 14b Paul
Cummings; 15t V. Belov; 16 Chris Hill; 17t Mark
Medcalf; 17b Tobyphotos; 18 Jack53; 19 Michal
Ninger; 20 Rafal Szozda; 21t Bildagentur Zoonar
GmbH; 21b Drakuliren; 11, 19t istock by Getty
Images

Cataloging-in-Publication Data

Names: Munson, Victoria.
Title: Birds / Victoria Munson.
Description: New York : Windmill Books, 2019. |
Series: My first book of nature | Includes glossary
and index.
Identifiers: LCCN ISBN 9781508196600 (pbk.)
| ISBN 9781508196594 (library bound) | ISBN
9781508196617 (6 pack)
Subjects: LCSH: Birds--Juvenile literature.
Classification: LCC QL676.2 M86 2019 | DDC
598--dc23

Manufactured in the United States of America

CPSIA Compliance Information: Batch #BS18WM:
For Further Information contact Rosen Publishing,
New York, New York at 1-800-237-9932

Contents

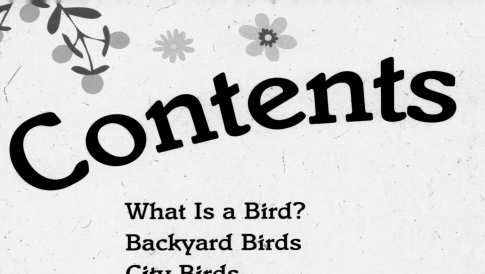

What Is a Bird?

Birds are warm-blooded animals that can lay eggs. A bird has feathers and wings. No other animal has feathers. Birds have a beak but no teeth.

Feathers are used to keep birds warm, help them to fly, and provide camouflage.

Most birds can fly. However, there are some birds that don't. These include penguins, ostriches, and kiwis.

4

Penguins are very strong swimmers, and ostriches are fast runners.

Ostriches can run at 60 mph (97 km/h)!

Penguins live at the cold South Pole.

Birds are found all over the world. Parrots are found in hot rainforests.

Flamingos live together in large groups near lakes and swamps.

Backyard Birds

Robins are small birds with bright red breasts. They love to sing from early in the morning to late at night.

Robins eat apples, nuts, and even spiders.

Male blackbirds have a bright yellow-orange beak.

Blackbirds eat worms, berries, and fruit.

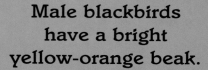

Mourning doves lay two eggs at a time. They can lay eggs up to six times a year. That's twelve baby mourning doves a year!

Cooo Coooo

Mourning doves make sad cooing sounds.

Juncos can be gray and white or reddish brown. They look for food by hopping and walking along the ground.

Juncos are snowbirds. They like winter!

City Birds

Male house sparrows have a black head and neck with white cheeks. Female sparrows are brown with no black markings.

Sparrows are very common in towns and cities.

Magpies are large **black and white birds.**

Magpie nests sometimes have roofs and two entrances. They have a loud chattering call.

chatter

chatter

8

Starlings live together in large flocks. A group of starlings is called a chattering.

Pigeons are the most common city bird. They are gray with shades of green and purple on their neck.

Starlings are very good at copying the sound of other birds, mammals, or even telephones!

Ring! Ring!

Pigeons live in large groups to protect themselves from predators such as cats, foxes, and rats.

Forest Birds

Song thrushes have heart-shaped brown spots on their cream-colored breasts. Mistle thrushes look very similar but are slightly larger.

Blue jays have bright blue feathers, white bellies, and pointy crests on their heads.

Blue jays are one of the loudest birds. Their call sounds like "Jay! Jay!"

Great spotted woodpeckers are black and white with a red patch under their tail.

Woodpeckers have two toes facing forward and two facing backwards.

Nuthatches are small, colorful birds with blue-gray wings and orange-brown breasts.

Nuthatches have a thick black line over each eye. Look for them walking upside down on hazel and beech trees.

11

Water Birds

Mallards live all over North America, Europe, and Asia. Male mallards have a green head, yellow beak, and white ring around their neck. Female mallards are speckled brown.

Don't feed ducks bread. It is bad for them. Instead, feed them seeds and berries.

Swans are very large white birds.

Swans have a long "S"-shaped neck. When angry, they will hiss and flap their wings.

Young swans are called cygnets.

Canada geese have long black necks and white cheeks. Large flocks of geese group together in parks and fields.

Look up to see these geese flying by in a "V" shape.

Canada geese can fly at 18 mph (30 km/h).

Moorhens are black with a red forehead. They live in ponds, rivers, and lakes. Their long green toes help them to grip on wet stones.

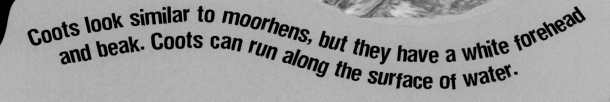

Coots look similar to moorhens, but they have a white forehead and beak. Coots can run along the surface of water.

13

Seabirds

Herring gulls are large, noisy birds. They have a red spot on their curved yellow beaks. When hungry chicks peck the red spot on the adult's beak, the adult knows to open its mouth and give food to its young.

In summer, black-headed gulls have black heads. For the rest of the year, their head has brown stripes. They like to live in groups.

Gulls eat fish, worms, and insects.

Oystercatchers have black and white bodies with long, bright orange beaks. They use their long beaks to open mussel shells.

Puffins live in groups on cliffs. They are black and white with a very colorful curved beak and bright orange legs.

Puffins eat tiny silver fish called sand eels.

Birds of Prey

Adult bald eagles have a dark brown body, and a white head and tail.

Eagles have a huge wingspan of over 6 feet (2 m).

Eagles have long, sharp talons for grabbing their prey.

Birds of prey sometimes perch on telephone poles along the road.

Sparrowhawks have a bar pattern across their chest. They do not hover like kestrels, but fly quickly, looking for small birds to eat.

The sparrowhawk's hooked beak helps it to scoop up prey.

Kestrels are small birds of prey with a long tail and pointed wings.

Kestrels eat small mammals such as mice and voles.

They hover above the ground before swooping down on their prey.

17

Owls

Barn owls have a snowy white breast and honey-colored back and wings. Their white face is heart-shaped.

Owls are usually nocturnal, which means they hunt at night, but barn owls can sometimes be seen in the daytime.

Look for barn owls in the early evening perched by the road. They are waiting to swoop down and catch mice and voles.

Long-eared owls are light brown with dark brown streaks. They get their name from their long ears! They have a dark brown, round face with orange eyes.

The male's loud hoot can be heard up to half a mile (1 km) away.

Hooot!

Short-eared owls have a brownish-black body, white face, and yellow eyes. Owls swallow their prey whole.

Short-eared owls can be seen hunting in the daytime.

19

Country Birds

Pheasants have long, beautiful tail feathers. Males are dark golden brown with a green head and red face wattles.

Females are paler brown and black. Pheasants live in fields.

Pheasants have excellent sight and hearing, which they use to help them avoid predators, such as foxes and birds of prey.

Redwings look like thrushes but have a bright red patch under their wings and a yellow stripe above their eyes.

In the fall, redwings fly in flocks of hundreds of birds.

Gray partridges have an orange face and mottled gray feathers. Their wings make a loud whirring noise when they fly.

Gray partridges lay one of the largest clutches of eggs in the world – 15 to 19 per nest!

Follow That Footprint

Sometimes it's hard to spot animals. Find out if a bird has been nearby by looking for clues.

In soft mud, birds will leave footprints behind.

Look at these footprints and see if you can spot any in your local wildlife habitat.

Moorhen

Bird of prey

Glossary and Index

camouflage colors on an animal's body that blend with the background, making it difficult to spot

predator an animal that hunts, kills, and eats other animals

prey an animal that is hunted and killed for food for another animal

warm-blooded having a body temperature that remains steady and warm, no matter what the outside temperature is. Mammals and birds are warm-blooded animals.